Pundemonium
Vol. 5

James E. Larson

Lefse Press—Agoura Hills, Ca
ISBN: 979-8-9874392-8-9
eBook ISBN: 979-8-9874392-9-6
Title: *Pundemonium Vol. 5*
Author: James E. Larson
Digital distribution | 2023
Paperback | 2023

Dedication

The author dedicates this book to his loving family, wife Cindy, daughter Erica, and son Greg. They have had to listen to the author over the years trying out the various puns on them. They deserve recognition for enduring that pun-ishment.

Chapter One

I heard in Texas a large western store that sells everything for horses is closing. The story is the new owner of the store had to borrow so much money from the bank to buy the store and to keep it stocked with all the merchandise. Then the economy went down and the customers stayed away.

In the end, the new owner of the horse apparel store was just saddled with too much debt.

An author had written a book about the history of the common eating utensil that has a long slender handle and which have around four tines at the end. When it came time to sell the book, the author put such a high price on the book which resulted in nobody buying the book. It seems nobody wanted to fork over that kind of money for such a book.

A wife asked her husband, who ran a small time furniture store, how did he know for my birthday I wanted a big piece of furniture with cabinets on top and a dresser below.

The husband said, "I just had a hutch!"

The thing about Chinese money is always yuan more.

A veterinarian once told me that fleas tend to group together at the base of the neck by the top of the front shoulders of a horse. He also added, usually after a while, the whole group just withers away.

I don't know if this is true or not, but I heard there is a Bollywood actor with the name of Curry Grant.

In England there is a Procrastinators Club that also participates in the Fox and Hounds hunting games.
When they start the hunt they yell, "Tarry Ho!"

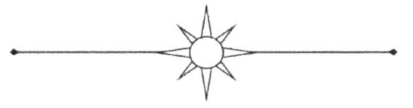

Chapter Two

Did you hear about the fisherman that was training a fairly large freshwater fish found throughout the States? He was training it to do underwater tricks and the fish seemed to always be eager to begin training in the very early mornings. You could say this fish processed a healthy dose of 'Carpe Diem!'

Just recently, a young man walked away from his job which was spending endless time running a tunneling machine for a new subway project. He said it was a just a boring job!

I just heard about a guy who loved giraffes so much he opened up a giraffe themed restaurant in Great Neck, New York. He even serves his wine in glass pitchers shaped like his favorite animal. The owner is very happy whenever you order a 'giraffe' of wine.

An old ex-boxer was being interviewed. The reporter asked the boxer how he got his nickname as the 'Mona Lisa' of Boxing. The reporter asked was it because of the beautiful and skillful way he boxed?

"No," said the boxer, "it was because after an opponent hit me with a knock-out punch, I spent almost as much time on canvas as the 'Mona Lisa' has!"

The National Association of Bicycle Wheels Manufacturing Companies just named a new spokesperson.

A farmer in Ohio just had produced a bumper crop of vegetables. He said he is going to change the type of vegetable grown next year and he hopes it will all turnip.

In Wisconsin, the CEO of the Dairy Association was being accused of being unfaithful to his wife because a photo of him kissing a woman was being circulated. In his defense, the CEO said he was so overworked and consumed with helping his dairy farmers increase milk production on their farms that he just lost control and kissed a stranger.

"Nonsense," said the CEO's secretary. She downplayed his distraction from helping the farmers and highlighted the kiss. His secretary basically threw her boss udder the buss.

Chapter Three

Did you know there is a Dental Hygienist Hall of Fame? All you have to do to get in is bring your own plaque!

It seems the critics of Ireland's Capital City will keep Dublin down in their assessment of the city.

A farmer who was harvesting his corn crop was getting ready to listen to the weather report on the radio because he was all ears.

I heard the story about twelve men and women who were sequestered in a jury trial and decided to order food in to save some time. They all wanted food with no seasoning but when it was delivered, it was seasoned. Talk about adding 'in salt to in jury!'

A young boy had a father with two sisters who were doctors and partners at a veterinarian clinic. They specialized in dogs that have heavy breathing problems which also make the dogs very nervous in addition to everything else. The nephew saw his dads two sisters work together one day and he said he could say for sure all the dogs had 'aunts in their pants!'

A factory worker that was making a rug on a loom was so drunk that he was weaving all over the place.

A small boat was sinking next to the dock in the harbor and the owner was rushing toward the boat to save it. At the same time, the harbor authorities were at the dock to seize the boat due to unpaid dock fees for over two years.

When the owner finally got there and saw all the commotion, he said, "I guess I'll be bailing out this boat one way or the other!"

A young kitchen helper's job in a famous Hollywood restaurant was to run small blocks of cheese across a metal blade that had many sharp holes in it. His mother always said, he was destined for grate-ness.

Chapter Four

There was a cake baking contest going on that had a baseball theme and many contestants were trying to come up with what to make. One guy thought his cake would not produce any big hit so he thought it was logical to just lay down a bunt cake and call it a day!

A locksmith was advertising for somebody to help him in his shop. He was looking for a key employee.

In Arizona, a new law that would prevent companies from selling counterfeit dentures was passed by the government but without any fines listed in the law. Ironically, the law to ban counterfeit dentures had 'no teeth in it!'

An animal scientist in the northern top of the world found two Arctic bears that had two distinct different behaviors and personalities. He declared they must be polar opposites.

A well-traveled tourist, who for some reason spoke only Pig Latin, had visited all the islands in the Philippines except one so he decided he would finally visit it. He thought that action was 'better Leyte than ever-nay!'

A taxidermist, who worked in his small shop, was known in the trade as a person who could restore stuffed animals that had somehow occurred damage to their fluffy/ bushy appendage at the rear of the animal. A reporter asked him once why doesn't he work in a large wholesale market that could give him more jobs and a chance to restore other parts of the animal.

The taxidermist replied, "I just prefer to work in my little shop and do retail."

There is going to be a new art gallery in New York that only showcases experimental art. I am told the owner of the gallery will start to hire people for security but the first requirement is that they already have to be Avant-Gardes.

The graduating class of students at the New Jersey Boxing School were trying to come up with what would be a fitting drink and the main course to serve at their graduation dinner. They came up with what they thought would be a good combination...Punch and Duck.

I just heard that tickets for the large shoe convention in Des Moines, Iowa have all been taken and the event is now all soled out.

At an outdoor cooking school, the staff just hired an ex-Marine as their official first Grill Instructor.

At a fishing convention near Hollywood, the people running the convention have planned some Hollywood themed contests and games. One that is planned is where the contestant stands with their fishing rod thirty feet from a table filled with fresh bakery items and the contestant has to try and hook a bun. They call this game 'Casting for a Role!'

The reason Peter Rabbit was never believed in court was because everything he said was all hare-say....

I watched a TV documentary on how the thin outside layer of metal is attached to the outside frame of an airplane. The reviewer said it was riveting.

A first year student at a Clown College in Florida, was excited after his first day at class. He was writing a letter to his parents to tell them about it. He said he might pledge the only fraternity on campus, which was Beta Omega Zeta Omega (which shortened to its first letters is BOZO). He also said he liked his clown-selor!

A clothing importer was walking along a clothing accessories bazaar in Singapore when he saw this booth that had all these brightly colored silk woman's head coverings. He thought they were beautiful and he better get them all before anybody else got them so he scarfed them up.

In England, an old man claims he can make owl sounds come out of his nose. Can he do it? Let's just let his nickname, which is 'Who Nose' answer that question.

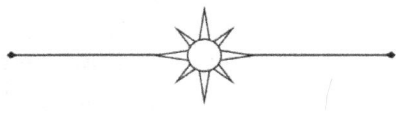

Chapter Five

I heard there is a small college in Minnesota that only enrolls students that want to become professional fisherman who want to compete for prizes in fishing tournaments. After a day of fishing, most of the students want to clean up, go to class, and debate what was left on their hook.

At a road building seminar, the next class for the students would cover how to build long drainage channels on both sides of the road. One student was heard saying he might not be going to that class. A fellow student heard him and said then don't go. The student replied, "You don't have to tell me how to avoid that class, I already know how to ditch it!"

A veterinarian by the name of Luke Watt had discovered a pill that would get rid of the mange in cats. He loved his cat so much that not only did he name his cat after his name, he then named the medicine after the cat's name. With all the money the veterinarian was earning on the new medicine, he bought an old hunting lodge in the local forest. Because he was so grateful for the pill for making him wealthy, he renamed the lodge after the name of the pill but he now thinks it was a bad idea. He says nobody wants to stay in a lodge when they hear the name which is 'Luke Watt the Cat Drug Inn.'

In a New York fashion show, I heard a group of critical fashion designers were upset that some fashions in the show were obviously out of date. There was talk that those fashion designers were going to remove those out-of-date fashions by forming a 'passe.'

I don't know if this is true or not, but I heard a wrestling organization in the south was going to finance a movie. They wanted it to showcase the various elements in wrestling. The plot was going to be about an old lady wrestler who teaches her young nephew how to be a great wrestler. The title for the movie will be 'Maim!'

I am told there is a castle guard at His Majesty's Fortress in London who everyone knows is always gloomy in his attitude on life. His fellow guards call him the 'Dour of London!'

Chapter Six

I am told there is a small basketball league in Switzerland that before every game they have a tradition of rubbing a thin coating of cheese over the ball. They use the kind of cheese that Switzerland is known for throughout the world. The ball does not make the same sound a regular ball makes when it hits nothing but net after going through the hoop...the cheese covered ball makes the sound 'Swiss!'

An old crane operator, who liked to travel, was digging in a gravel pit and loading up a dump truck. He noticed that the thing that scoops up the gravel was not level, one side was way up and one side was way down. He thought while the crane would be in for repairs, he would do some things he had been wanting to accomplish in his life. This was all going to happen because of his bucket list.

A couple were debating whether or not to go to a local prison for a program to hear some of their residents recite their original poetry. The husband said the decision to go to the prison for that program would involve 'Prose and Cons.'

Did you hear the musical group the Black Eyed Peas might get their own podcast?

A man sent his brother, who he didn't like very well but did not want to tell him directly, on an errand down to the dock. He was told to purchase from this very short vendor, who came from the same background as the brothers, what the vendor was selling. The vendor was selling a one foot wide by four foot long metal pan in which people usually cook oriental food. So what the brother who told the brother on the errand what to do was to take a long wok off a short peer.

I had heard our local drapery store was going out of business. When I contacted the owner and asked him why, he said, "Our suppliers could not supply us with our main product, which is curtains for us!"

Chapter Seven

A Synagogue had a couple of congregants that were ornithologists who specialized in the rehabilitation of injured owls. They opened up a salon for owls and they claimed it was the best in the world. That kind of attitude led to the name of the salon which they named 'HootSpa!'

Marv and another guy named Les were bidding against each other at an art auction over a piece of art. The seller was so happy because the bids were getting very high. The seller was told to expect a large sum of money from somebody.

"That would be Marv or Les," said the seller.

A detective at a police station in New York was receiving quite the reputation for getting confessions out of suspected criminals. He recently got one out of a really emaciated super model that was on track to inherit a massive fortune but in the meantime, the woman was accused of a burglary. The detective was unsure if the confession would stand up in court because the woman's attorney could say he tricked the suspect and pulled the confession out of the thin heir.

Did you know there is a new book out all about crows and the author is Raven all about it?

Somebody told me crows can never get a fair break in any courtroom in the country. Even if they are innocent, whenever a group of crows get together in a courtroom, somebody will stand up and point to them and yell, "There's a murder now!"

In Austria, a couple of butchers were having a contest about who made the better sausage. They hired the judges to select the winner when they had finished making the sausage. Unbeknown to one butcher, the other butcher had bribed the judges because he was desperate to come out on top and he wanted to win in the wurst way.

Sometimes, when a small rectangular piece of paper you stick on the upper right corner of an envelope is released at the post office and it becomes very popular, the postal workers at the counter brace themselves for a stampede.

Chapter Eight

Did you know sometimes there are chickens who in the afterlife turn into mischievous ghosts that often roam the hen house. They are called 'Poultrygeists!'

A cowboy tailor in Hollywood known for his fancy rhinestone covered suits, was showing a new creation to the press. The new creation had a suit coat and pants covered in rhinestones and lights. The owner told the press, "You haven't seen anything yet!"

He went onto say, "The vest is yet to come!"

Having dark brown hair dye running down your face after applying it on your balding head, is in some societies, an example of having a pate worse than death.

An overworked shoe salesman was working in a shoe store called 'The Foot.'

One day I guess he snapped and he proceeded to put on a new pair of shoes, took cash from the register, and then fled the scene. Unbeknown to him, his boss was going to give him a raise, but not any more after this incident. A local reporter had this as the next day's headline, 'Upset Local Shoe Salesman Shod Himself in THE FOOT.'

Do you think a criminal walking down a staircase in a courtroom making disparaging remarks about the judge, is an example of a condescending action by the criminal?

Do you know the main reason why they frown on putting dried straw on the roofs in parts of old England anymore? Because of fire, thatch why!

A belt designer loved to bid at storage container auctions to seek materials to work with in his shop. A recent bin had lots of leather in it plus a few coils of rope. Rather than throw the rope away, he made some rope belts that had a very decorative knot where the rope ends met. When he put a photo of the belts on his website, many orders came pouring in to his shop. He advertised his belt with the slogan, "Waist Knot, Want Knot!"

Chapter Nine

An arrogant TV producer had a show which only featured people who had inherited a lot of money. He was always putting on heirs.

A scatterbrained comedian had a gimmick that he would knit things while he told jokes. He was billed as a self-confessed 'Knit Wit!'

I bought a ticket and went to a Bob Marley concert years ago. I paid the reggae-lar price.

It only seems logical that the least sophisticated members of King Arthur's other court were the Knights of the Square Table.

The men's underwear factory's president was wanting to expand his line of product. The stockholders said no and wanted the president to notify the public when he briefs the press.

The young mother had a talk with her young son, a second grader, before he left for school. She said don't get drawn into fights and be a good boy. She wrote a note and put it in his sack lunch. At the bottom of the piece of paper was the advice which was the best part of the sack lunch. She wrote the note which was the 'P.S. Resist Taunts!'

Strawberry Festivals are always very popular but they always seem end up with a traffic jam.

Last Halloween, I heard there was store in Hollywood that only sold Halloween items but they could not find enough people to work there. The store could only provide a skeleton crew.

A guy went to a boat ramp in a marina to put his boat in the water. The sign near the boat ramp said there was no charge to back the boat trailer into the water but there would be a twenty dollar charge to pull the trailer out of the water. The boat owner said to his son, "You see son, there is no such thing as a free launch!"

Chapter Ten

A musical instrument store owner had two big bass drums with broken drum heads in his back storeroom. The owner could not sell them as is so he stacked one atop the other, screwed them together, and put a small granite slab on top. He took that to his brother's furniture store and sold it. The musical store owner said, "Well if you can't beat them, join them!"

A marathon race was going to be held on a large Navy base near Los Angeles. One Navy officer for the race thought one large portable toilet facility was enough. Another officer thought there should be one more. He said, "Two heads are always better than one!"

I heard a pillow factory in Indiana that still uses duck feathers was laying off quite a few employees. I think you would call that an example of downsizing.

Somebody told me that when the Terminator is between projects, he works at a grocery store as a box boy. People get a kick when they ask him on what aisle are the paper towels and are they toward the front of the store or toward the back. The Terminator always says, "Aisle B back!"

Near Colorado Springs, Colorado there is a famous mountain called Pikes Peak. A ninety year old resident of the City finally hiked to the top of the mountain, and when he got there he slammed his fist into the snow. When asked what took him so long to accomplish this feat, he said, "I didn't want to hit my peak too early in life!"

I am told there was a little known gladiator that fought in the Colosseum in Rome. He would turn around and run backwards with his large firm backside into his opponent, knock him to the ground and then sit on his chest and knock the wind out of him. His name was 'Gluteus Maximus....'

A new World War II movie is coming out from Germany with the dialogue in German. It is about the kind of ships that travel underwater so it makes sense the movie has subtitles.

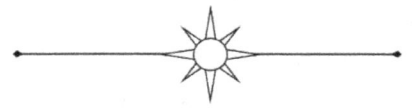

Chapter Eleven

A strange thing happened at a small town college in Oklahoma. A student wrestler pinned himself in a wrestling match as he had been trying to learn how to 'hold one's own' during the match.

A toothbrush factory in Texas was accused by the state Attorney General of using unsafe fibers in the head of their toothbrushes. The owner of the factory bristled at the accusation.

An aircraft supply store that among many items, sells altimeter gauges, which are the gauges that tells the pilot how high the airplane is off the ground. Unfortunately, they were taken off the shelves because they were found to be defective. The store owner said the gauges just did not measure up....

One of the countries around the Mediterranean Sea have been trying new tourist slogans. One of the first they came up with is 'There Are No Squeaking Wheels in Greece!'

A criminal in a downtown courthouse in Los Angeles threatened a witness in one of his cases that was to come before a judge. He threatened her with a knife. He was arrested under the charge of 'Con-kniving' to commit a crime.

A man who was tired of living with his financial income fluctuating up and down all year long decided to buy a business that boards horses in a large barn. He said at least now I will have a stable income.

At a booth at a vintage clothing convention, a man had a display board he had rushed to be completed for the convention. The display showed the different styles of men's zippers in clothing through the years. He was asked if he had any other exhibits he had done like that for the convention and he said, "No, I just did this one on the fly!"

At a local automobile junk yard, the owner of the car crusher machine that compresses cars down to about a couple of feet in height, was asked by a reporter if it made him sad to see cars end up like that. "Not at all," he said flatly...

Chapter Twelve

In Louisiana, a man spent considerable time training his pet flamingo to run very fast. When the flamingo was in its best shape, the man would challenge owners of other animals to a race of 100 yards with the winner collecting a small bet. The man thought having a well-trained flamingo would give him a leg up on the competition.

A factory that produces the product that comes from dried grapes wanted to increase the public awareness of the health benefits of their product. The advertising company they hired said they were going to be dedicated to raisin excitement levels in the public.

The young ballerina dancer was always alert and ready for any new direction given to her by her instructor. She was always on her toes.

The dog with a very bad case of fleas was itching to go to the veterinarian.

In Minnesota there are a number of towns with a large Mr. Bunyon and the Blue Ox statues throughout the state. They always seem to cast a Paul throughout the town.

Before the farmers could enter their pig in the pig races at their local county fair, they would have to add their pig to the swine-up list.

An optometrist wanted to change careers late in life so he became an elementary school teacher. People asked him if it was a big change.

"Not really," he said, "I am still dealing with pupils!"

I just watched a very good nature film about frogs. It was ribbiting!

I heard that many years ago in the frontier days of the old west, women would sometimes get tired of their men smelling like horses. So the women would send away for bars of soap with different scents in them. I was told this action was an example of the first use of a 'Male Odor Catalog.'

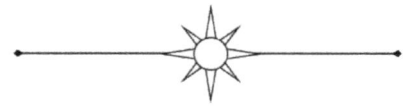

Chapter Thirteen

A butcher in New York had two passions in life besides being a butcher. One was the photographs taken by the famous photographer who took the photographs of Yosemite National Park and the other passion was the use of the names of fairy tales in everyday life. When he would sell a package of steaks, he would include a copy of one of those park photographs. He named this special offer 'Ansel and Gristle.'

In Oregon, a vocal coach who judges many singing contests throughout the state, was cutting down some large trees on his property. However, instead of yelling out the word that is most associated with a lumberjack as a tree falls, the vocal coach would yell, "TIMBRE!"

An executive with a company that makes window panes, stood up at a stockholders meeting and said their product is not the best in the business and the product needs to improve. Some of the other executives thought he had just committed 'Glassphemy!'

Archaeologists in England recently discovered there was an ancient civilization that worshiped apples which they thought had magical powers. This was their core belief.

On Broadway in New York, auditions were being conducted to find the right horse to appear on stage for the play Oklahoma. One horse tripped getting on stage and broke his leg, but the producer felt so bad he decided to fix his leg by having someone put a 'Plaster of Paris' support item around the leg. The horse's owner bragged to everyone this was the first time that a horse was ever in a cast on Broadway! The play's director was overheard saying that was a lame joke.

Superman needed a replacement for the cloth item that hangs from the back of his neck and flows behind him when he flies. Superman asked all of the tailors that he interviewed if they could make one...if they were capable?

Chapter Fourteen

There are some people who think an old stem winding clock with a second hand would on earth make a different sound on the moon due to the lessor amount of gravity on the moon. The people who are researching that possibility are called luna-tics.

Two camping enthusiasts were discussing in front of an audience, which piece of camping equipment was the most important to have in their backpack. One said a canteen. The other person said a kitchen utensil called a sieve. According to the audience poll taken shortly afterward, by an overwhelming majority, the audience agreed that the canteen was the most important and that the argument for the sieve just did not hold water.

A student Oceanographer was taking a test where one of the problems was to convert the depth of the ocean in feet to the depth of the ocean in a nautical term. He was having a hard time to fathom that.

A tennis equipment supply store was conducting a promotion where they were having a drawing for a free basic tennis racket with no strings attached.

Up near the Arctic Circle there is a saloon that upon entering will dry your wet snowy jacket for a fee as long as you hang it on the Parka meter.

A cooking show TV producer loved the movie 'The Sound of Music' so much that his desire was to parody the songs in that movie and have them performed on his TV show. The first song was about the correct way to use the kitchen utensil that has a long handle that terminates into a deep bowl and used for soups and stews. He titled the song 'Ladle-wise.'

A guy I know loves to eat nuts all day. When I asked him what is his favorite nut was and when did he start doing this, he replied it Pecan a long time ago.

I heard there is a factory in Indiana that makes glue where all the factory workers went on strike. The management team tried to get the workers to go back to work but the workers said they made a decision and they are going to stick to it.

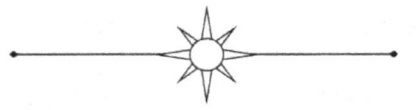

Chapter Fifteen

Atrainer of birds found along California's southern beaches was asked by a motion picture company to come to their movie set. They wanted to discuss using of some of the birds he has trained in a film. The trainer met with them and said when you hire the birds Heron you hire me.

Somebody told me there was a pirate long, long ago with a wooden leg named Smith. History never told us what the name of the other leg was...but this pirate with a wooden peg leg was a member of a group of other peg leg pirates that loved to dance. One day this pirate after a day of dancing, which almost shattered his peg leg, broke away from this group and started his own splinter party.

There was a robbery at a factory that makes bathroom scales. The cops were chasing the suspect but he jumped on a scale and got a weigh.

A young pastor was going to be assigned to a new area in a state. Somebody asked him what would happen if he was selected to go to a new neighborhood church area where he did not want to be assigned.

"Well," he said, "I would Parrish the thought!"

In an old restaurant in China, a cook in the kitchen who was using the large metal bowl they use for cooking, was also trying to quit chewing so much gum every day. He was trying to wok and eschew gum at the same time.

There were a pair of comedians who worked as fishermen on a boat during the day and did their comedy at night at a seafood restaurant. They called their act, based on their jokes about their day jobs, 'The Fish Shticks!'

The person who invented 'Holograms' made one of himself but he was having problems with it and it made him mad. He was beside himself!

A Zoologist was studying both animal behavior and human behavior for a particular thesis. He found that humans make more mistakes than animals and that cows in particular don't mind if humans do wrong to them. The title of his book on the subject was "To Err Is Human, To Forgive, Bovine!"

Chapter Sixteen

The Broadway Musical 'CATS' had a long run on Broadway in New York. Little known fact is that when it opened, the play's producers thought it would be cute if they named the area in front of the ticket booth, where people would buy tickets, the 'Fee Line!'

A documentarian film maker made a film on the history of writing instruments used in the years prior to the use of goose feathers. Since he covered the area of history before the use of goose feathers, he called his film a prequill.

Believe it or not, I heard that at a small University in Utah, the student bookstore has for sale for the student course on Mountain Climbing a corresponding Cliffs Notes book.

I was told that the owner of the horse used in a local rodeo for the bucking bronco contest keeps a tally of all of the cowboy riders that have been thrown off by the horse. The owner calls it the horse's 'Bucket List!'

Some of you may remember years ago when Roy Rogers' horse died, some newspapers coverage of the event came with a 'Trigger Warning!'

Most everyone knows that the Korean War Themed TV show named MASH was an acronym for Mobil Army Surgical Hospital. But there was a piece of equipment that they also needed and when they ordered the hospital they also ordered this piece of equipment. It was the Portable Oblong Table Available To Operate Everywhere Simply. When they put the two acronyms together, the Army Doctors Request Form would say we need 'MASH POTATOES!'

A carpenter heard about an unbelievable sale on carpenter tools at a store. He wasn't sure if that was a store he could trust to tell the truth and he was also unsure which tools were included in the sale. He was looking for that tool that you lay atop a horizontal wood beam to see if both ends of the beam are at the same elevation. He really wanted to see if that sale was on the level.

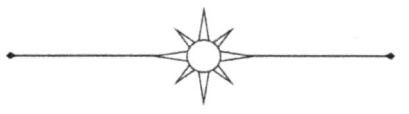

Chapter Seventeen

I heard when he was younger, in order to make ends meet, a future German composer worked in a mine in Germany. One day he discovered a small vein of silver but suddenly some of the silver fell on him and knocked him down. He lived near the mine so his mother was called and she helped remove the rocks off her son. When the rocks were off, his mother said, "Well, that's a lode of my Bach!"

A long time ago a psychic decided to open a steak house in uptown New York with the name of the restaurant being 'Meat-Up-Town!' The prices were very good and the psychic personally cooked every steak. However, no matter how you ordered your steak done at the table, all the steaks came out of the kitchen as Medium cooked.

Somebody told me a writer wrote a sequel to the book, "A Tree Grows in Brooklyn." The writer called his new book, "A Shrub Grows in Yonkers." All the critics thought the new book was 'bush league!"

There was a building contractor who spent his time restoring old run-down houses. He became emotionally attached every time he started work on a house trying to bring the house back to its past glory. The name of his company was called 'Dwelling in the Past!'

I think people figure out answers to most of their problems in the very early morning because during that time period is when things dawn on you.

A robber was convicted and sentenced to a mountain top prison in Kentucky. This prison had an adjacent chicken egg laying business that employed some of their inmates. While there, the robber secretly made a glider plane disguised as a hen house. One night when the glider was finished, he pushed it off the side of the mountain and left the prison. Headlines in the newspapers the next day said the prisoner 'Flew the Coop!'

An ornithologist who was always very high up in trees looking for unique birds' nests was always going out on a limb.

Chapter Eighteen

In the Northeastern United States, there are Indian Tribes that at their ancestral homelands have very tall poles with many faces carved into them from top to the bottom of the pole. Haven't you ever wondered how many faces are on one pole in totum?

Somebody told me that when he was younger, SpongeBob SquarePants got a lot of traffic violations, but now his lawyers have expunged his records.

It has been said that whenever the well-known contortionist twisted himself into the shape of eyeglasses, he was making a spectacle of himself.

The board of directors at a factory that makes drapes for windows were considering branching out into a window cover that has wood slats in it. The president of the company asked for a voice vote of ayes or nays. When it came his turn, only one director voted for the new covering. You could say he was the only one who turned a blind aye toward the possible new product.

A group of old plumbers in London formed a dance club. When asked by a bystander what kind of dance does the public like, one plumber piped up and said, "Clog Dancing is very popular!"

The owner of a swimming pool installation company had one of his key employees call in sick. The employee was an expert in installing the 12" wide concrete ring around the edge of the pool at the pool deck level. The owner took over his employee's job and he said was coping as best as he could.

A guy was driving around in the dark, lost in a neighborhood he did not recognize. All of a sudden, his front wheel fell off and it made a loud noise.

A man in a house came out and asked the guy what happened. The driver said, "I think I lost my bearings and I don't know where I am!"

About the Author

The author, James E. Larson, has always enjoyed a good pun. Just recently, he decided to create new ones for a book. He says like anything else, some puns come easy while other need some rewrites before they are finished. A good pun needs a good back story that sets up the 'Pun-ch Line.' That is the fun part of creating puns.

Printed in the USA
CPSIA information can be obtained
at www.ICGtesting.com
LVHW090319270424
778611LV00001B/133

9 798987 439289